How to Work with Self-Publishers
Editing, proofreading and other considerations

Alison Shakspeare

First published in the UK in 2021 by
Chartered Institute of Editing and Proofreading
Apsley House
176 Upper Richmond Road
London
SW15 2SH

ciep.uk

Copyright © 2021 Chartered Institute of Editing and Proofreading

ISBN 978 1 915141 00 2 (print)
ISBN 978 1 915141 01 9 (PDF ebook)

All rights reserved. No part of this publication may be reproduced or used in any manner without written permission from the publisher, except for quoting brief passages in a review.

The moral rights of the author have been asserted.

The information in this work is accurate and current at the time of publication to the best of the author's and publisher's knowledge, but it has been written as a short summary or introduction only. Readers are advised to take further steps to ensure the correctness, sufficiency or completeness of this information for their own purposes.

Developmental editing, copyediting and proofreading by CIEP members
Margaret Hunter, Cathy Tingle, Ian Howe and Bev Sykes

Typeset in-house
Original design by Ave Design (avedesignstudio.com)
Image credits: 1 Pixabay/Geralt, 23 Shutterstock/pathdoc, 30 Shutterstock/StepanPopov, 37 Pixabay/Jessica Ruscello

Contents

1 | Introduction	1
The publishing landscape	3
The publishing workflow	5
Overview of an editor's role	7
2 | Assessing the author's needs	10
Author's knowledge	10
Author's mindset	12
Author's budget	14
Author's timescale	22
Connecting with the author	22
Key questions when assessing an author	24
3 | The practicalities	27
Text preparation	27
Content issues	30
Formatting for layout	32
Anatomy of a book	34
Choosing a format	35
About ISBNs	41
About metadata	44
Book distribution	45

4 | Additional professional services   47
    Indexers   47
    Illustrators/cover designers   49
    Book layout   51
    Marketing and publicity   51
    Agents   52

5 | Resources   53

About the author   57

1 | Introduction

A boom in book self-publishing has increased work for editors and, given that self-publishers have a range of skills and technical abilities, this has opened a host of opportunities for editors to develop services that self-publishers will want to pay for. This overview of self-publishing also drills down into more technical details for those who want to be aware of the issues self-publishers will face throughout the process.

This guide is for practising editors who want to develop their support of self-publishing authors, in fiction and non-fiction. There are many aspects of the process you may never need, or want, to deal with, but knowing how they work will help you assess a client's assumptions, answer their questions and be of service in guiding them towards a professional self-publication. You may even encounter parts of the process that you'd like to develop as a business service, and this guide should help you work out what skills and knowhow you need to invest in.

This 'Introduction' looks at the publishing landscape and reflects on how self-publishing mirrors or differs from more traditional publishing routes. It then outlines the standard publishing workflow and describes the editor's role within it.

Chapter 2, 'Assessing the author's needs', is about getting a feel for the author's skills and knowledge, which should help you decide on the sort of work you could or should offer them – or whether you ought to take on the project at all, from both budgetary and skills angles.

Chapter 3, 'The practicalities', runs through the technicalities of turning a manuscript into a book, from what the editor adds, to what an ISBN does, to thinking about metadata and book distribution. This chapter is heavy on detail that you may never need to know if you are offering a single service, but it sheds some light on what happens once a manuscript has left your tender mercies – and some of you may choose to tread further along that path.

Some of the paths to self-publication may look a little different from traditional publishing, but they are still governed by the philosophy that creating a book worth reading, whether in print or as an ebook, is a team effort. Chapter 4 on 'Additional professional services' describes what each person or service could bring to the table, such as creative design or thorough indexing. This is also the chapter that could give you ideas on what new skills you might acquire to extend your service offering.

Since an author needs to understand all the publishing processes if they are going to use their time and money wisely and appropriately, then it can only help if you too understand the whole picture. The world of self-publishing is expanding all the time. This guide is based on experiences up to the time of writing, but even six months after publication technological developments and a growth in service providers will have changed the landscape. While your core editing skills will always be the foundation of your business, if you want to help self-publishers find their way you'll need to keep in touch with how polished manuscripts are being turned into books for sale. You might find that much of the detail in this guide is superfluous to your own requirements, but an enquiring author could find it useful and you may wish to pass that information on.

Links to organisations or tools referred to within the text are listed in the 'Resources'. Some entries will be useful for many years, others will soon be superseded, while some no-shows will surprise you because they'll have sprung up after this guide's been published.

The publishing landscape

The landscape contains reputable and trustworthy publishers and service providers, as well as the less experienced or professional (see table 1, '**The publishing landscape**', for an overview). To make wise choices an author should ask for recommendations, sign up to author networks on social media, compare service offerings and use vetted directories.

A strong recommendation for self-publishing authors, and for editors who work with them, is to join the **Alliance of Independent Authors** (ALLi). This is a global organisation with a strong presence in the UK and the US. It lobbies on behalf of independents, it produces an annual directory of approved and rated services, and it is an active network for keeping abreast of changes in and ideas for production and marketing. Members have access to a wealth of publications that go way beyond this guide. If you are accepted as a Partner Member (vetted professionals) you get an entry in the ALLi directory and gain another source of work.

If a book is a one-off and the author is inexperienced then they will need to use/pay for more services. If the author has grander plans then they will have to absorb more information. The appropriate decision will depend on how entrepreneurial the author is (see table 3, '**Author mindset**') and whether the book is for limited, personal distribution or is aimed at a wider audience. If you can offer additional skills (perhaps as an indexer), or recommendations or trusted partners (typesetters or illustrators), then you'll be adding value to your service offering.

Table 1 The publishing landscape

Common descriptor	Type of organisation	Services
Trade publishers	Dominated by the big names of Penguin Random House, Hachette Livre, HarperCollins and Macmillan Publishers, but covering such familiar names as Oxford University Press and Scholastic	• Authors generally come to traditional publishers through an agent; they sign a contract, may get an advance and receive royalties • The publisher manages the production process and does the marketing and distribution • The author has very little control
Independent publishers	Thousands of small presses across all genres, from Countryside Books to the Royal Armouries	• Operate much like the big companies for author contracts and process management, but are generally specialists • Can be more approachable than larger publishers; can require more manuscript preparation and marketing from the author
Self-publishing services	Freelance individuals offering one or more services (eg CIEP members) Or companies that handle multiple services for a fee (eg BookBaby or Matador)	• Authors choose and pay for the services they require; can maximise control and income • Service providers should create a professional product; some promise more than they deliver; some charge over and above for print copies

Common descriptor	Type of organisation	Services
Vanity presses	Once a term for all publishing that was funded by an author rather than a trade publisher; now used to describe publication services that prioritise their own profits	• Companies sell minimal services for maximum fee; authors are often left with a badly produced product and no rights or income
Self-publishing platforms	These are print on demand (POD) and ebook distribution services and the principal players are Amazon KDP, Apple, IngramSpark and Lulu	• Self-publishing authors can have their own accounts with all such platforms to maximise control over pricing and to improve marketing, but they need a professional product to upload

The publishing workflow

The self-publishing process is not that different from traditional publishing, but the author is the manager with overall creative direction, not least because they hold the purse strings. But they should not expect to carry out all the tasks. If the end result is going to be a professional publication then the author needs to gather a good team. Figure 1 on the next page outlines the traditional publishing workflow in a general grouping and timing of tasks. You can see your editorial role firmly at the start, but note those other processes that occur concurrently or need planning for – and which the author might thank you for flagging up.

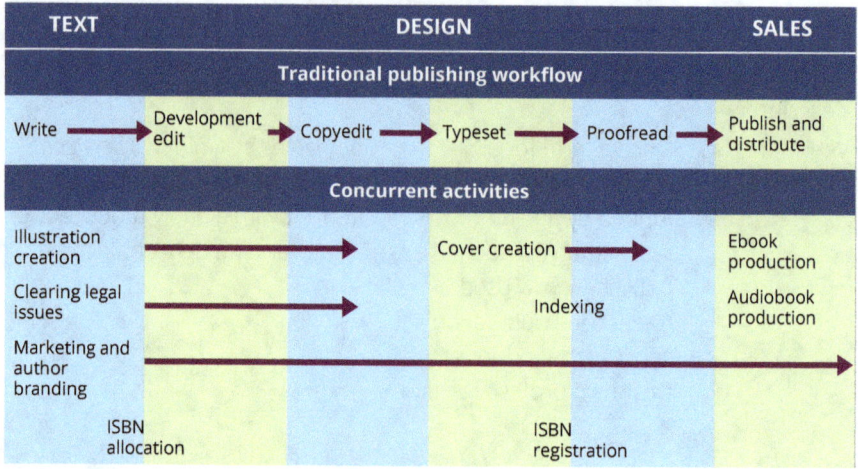

Figure 1 Traditional publishing workflow

The process falls roughly into:

1. text preparation
2. book design and production
3. sales and marketing.

Some activities need thinking about well before they need to be in place and others can't happen until earlier stages are complete. For instance:

- Traditional indexes are compiled from page proofs produced after layout, but since good indexers can be booked up months ahead don't leave it to the last minute to look for one (see '**Indexers**' in chapter 4).
- ISBNs are cheaper if bought in bulk, and publishing names need to be set up in order to buy them, but individual ISBNs can only be registered as active after each book format is produced because of the details needed, such as trim size and number of pages (see '**About ISBNs**' in chapter 3).
- It adds to the cost and can create confusion if a book is laid out/ typeset before all the editing is complete and the subsidiary material is gathered.

1 | Introduction

Overview of an editor's role

As an editor you play a key role in preparing the text, but once you understand what self-publishing entails you could add value to your business by:

- making authors aware of the choices that are available
- advising authors on those things that *have* to be done
- expanding your role and skill set within the self-publishing process – or setting up partnerships (see table 2, '**Publishing roles**').

As a professional copyeditor you will be familiar with your role in checking:

- clarity, coherence and consistency of content
- inclusive and accessible language
- text formatting
- copyright and legal issues
- references and illustrations.

As a professional proofreader you'll know about scrutinising for:

- content consistency
- layout issues.

> **If the end result is going to be a professional publication then the author needs to gather a good team.**

Table 2 Publishing roles

Aspect of publishing	Editor's role	Other roles
State of the text	The same process as with any new editing project: is it still at development stage, will it need a thorough copyedit, or is it ready to proofread?	• Beta readers
Supporting material: prelims (inc. ISBN, copyright information) and endmatter (such as an index); illustrations; cover	An editor often indicates the placement of/need for some of these in the manuscript; some of these processes you might be able to help with, but the author needs to prepare for/invest in all of them	• Illustrator • Designer • Indexer • Typesetter
Legal issues related to libel, permissions and copyright	Issues commonly come up during editing if the text contains quotes, illustrations or references to living persons, but, given how long this process can take, it is worth establishing the author's awareness of the issues and whether they've already done the work	• Permissions editor
Getting the book 'out there'	Is the author aware of the restrictions/possibilities of various self-publishing routes? Can you help them decide? Knowing the destination helps with manuscript preparation/formatting	• Self-publishing service provider • Printer • Distributor • Marketing support
Process management	Is the author prepared or equipped to manage the process themselves or might they need a project manager/competent computer user?	• Self-publishing service provider • Marketing support

As an experienced editor working with a self-publisher it can also be helpful if you:

- get a clear picture of what the author wants to do with the manuscript (just produce an ebook or also a paperback, for example)
- are clear about what they expect you to do/help with, over and above your usual editing tasks – and are willing to pay for
- are extra rigorous about formatting for design and layout, particularly if the author is planning to use an online template service
- offer suggestions for project planning by asking the author if they have
  » booked an indexer/illustrator (see '**Indexers**' in chapter 4)
  » sourced a cover designer (see '**Illustrators/cover designers**' in chapter 4)
  » bought ISBNs (see '**About ISBNs**' in chapter 3)
  » selected a publication route (see '**Book distribution**' in chapter 3).

Sales and marketing will probably be the most difficult area for you to help with unless you have the right experience – book marketing is a far cry from promoting an editing business. If your author only wants to produce a few books for their family or their club then this won't come into it. If they have grand plans for an exciting series then they will certainly need advice (and maybe you can give them some pointers, at the very least to follow successful authors' blogs or Facebook group discussions). But the main message you have to get across is that marketing is up to the author – and that the earlier they think about it the better. Unless they have the budget to pay for a service, they will have to be prepared to invest plenty of their own time and considerable effort to achieve sales.

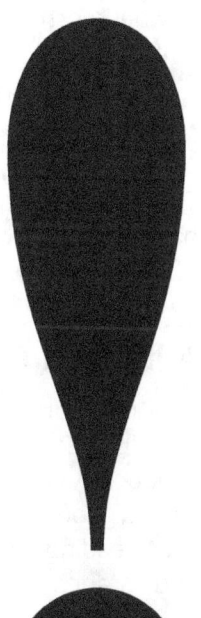

2 | Assessing the author's needs

This is a key step in deciding whether to take on an author as a client and what you can offer. As any practising editor knows, first-time authors can be wearing rose-tinted spectacles when it comes to their manuscript's readability, and this also applies to its publishability. So, however they describe what they think they need, you must see a representative sample of their writing and use your editor's knowledge to gauge what needs to be done (first by you, and then by other service providers) to make it publication ready.

You also need a bigger picture to clarify the advice you might need to give, the amount of work that might be needed, and to forge a good relationship with your author. It will help if you can establish:

- the extent of their knowledge about publishing processes
- whether they have an introspective or an entrepreneurial mindset
- if they have a sensible budget in mind
- if they are working to a realistic timescale
- that you are communicating in the same language and will connect.

The following touches on what each of these entails, but don't feel you have to bombard your potential client with all this at once. There's a list of key questions at the end of this chapter.

Author's knowledge

Your initial query should be: is this your first book? If the answer is yes, then further questions will reveal how much they really know about producing a book, as opposed to what they've always assumed. And it's always good to deal with false assumptions early in a project (such as proofreading being the same thing as copyediting; or thinking bookshops and libraries will order books through Amazon).

Nothing will replace actually seeing the manuscript, but delicate questions about what they've written before (whether during their education, for work or purely for pleasure), or even whether they've read much of the genre they've written in, can indicate their awareness of what makes something worth publishing. If they are writing for a specialist non-fiction market, then their knowledge of and standing in that field should indicate the quality of the content and help with target marketing. If they have produced genre fiction but don't read that genre then you may need to introduce them to what those readers expect, which can be very specific in certain genres such as romance or young adult fiction.

> This is my first book; I have always had stories in my head ... I now have time to fulfil my lifelong dream and put pen to paper ... I rarely read fiction and certainly not women's novels.
>
> A would-be author, whose manuscript was unpublishable but who carried on writing for personal enjoyment

The next useful question is about who else has read the manuscript. Fond family members and friends are less likely to have been usefully critical than writing group members, beta readers or other editors.

Even if this is the author's nth book (self-published or not), their understanding of editing, book production and publication may not match yours, or may be incomplete. Useful discussion points are:

- on editing – do they understand consistency; have they heard of style sheets; do they know about, and use, Track Changes?
- on book production – are they aware of copyright; have they found a typesetter/book designer; what formats are they planning to produce?
- on publication – have they got ISBNs; do they have a POD account; have they got a website?

> The most valuable thing my editor does is listen to me when I tell her what I want her to do. I know the areas that I need help with, and I know those things – usually matters of style – that I've made my decision on and don't need highlighting.
>
> Kevin Partner, self-published author

Author's mindset

If the author tells you that their aim is to find a mainstream publisher or an agent, then they aren't in the self-publishing zone – yet. Although, you could point out that many publishers pick up 'new' authors after seeing sales figures from successful self-publishers.

Table 3 lists some common drivers for wanting to self-publish and flags up the services the author is most likely to benefit from. It also shows that the more entrepreneurial their approach, the more services an author will need – or the more skills/knowledge they will need to acquire.

Table 3 Author mindset

Driver	Are they looking to sell?	Services required
It's a cathartic exercise	Want it professionally edited but don't want to make it publicly available (not a self-publisher)	• Editing
It's a family souvenir	For private consumption only	• Editing • Layout* • Printing
Club anniversary	To members only	• Editing • Layout* • [ISBN optional, but valuable] • Printing

2 | Assessing the author's needs

Driver	Are they looking to sell?	Services required
Business development	Yes, as part of their business development/support (therefore the marketing is likely to be part of their business)	- Editing - Layout* and ebook formatting - ISBNs - Printing/POD account - Marketing copywriter
I've written this novel/these short stories	Yes	- Editing - Layout* and ebook formatting - ISBNs - Printing/POD account - Marketing†
I want to have/gain control of my work	Yes	- Editing - Layout* and ebook formatting - ISBNs - Printing/POD account - Marketing†

Note: * layout = cover, illustrations, typesetting; † marketing = website, social media, book launch etc

If the author's main driver is to control their work then they need the technical ability to cope with the range of online processes and bits of software that enable self-publishing. It is useful to get a handle on whether their desire to do it themself is matched by their technical abilities and their willingness to learn. If they are flummoxed by computers then they will have to adjust their expectations – and increase their budget.

Author's budget

As in all walks of life, you get what you pay for, and publishing is as prone to rip-offs as any business. Many an author has become a self-publisher because of an experience with a packager who has cost them a few thousand pounds, only to leave them with 20 books and little if no income from sales.

If an author is willing to learn about and manage the technicalities themself there is no doubt that they can save a lot of money and earn greater rewards, but they have to be comfortable dealing with online processes and bureaucracy. If they are not skilled in using the required technology or software then they have to be willing to pay someone to end up with a good product that their public can find and buy.

Each step has its own rates and requirements. If the author is unwilling to invest the bare minimum in even a thorough copyedit, say £500, then they are not being realistic. It is not sensible to attempt to give a basic cost to produce 'a book' because so much depends on the state of its contents and its size, but table 4 lists some suggested professional rates and basic costs by publication stage and indicates how different decisions can impact the budget.

2 | Assessing the author's needs

Table 4 Budgeting (based on UK examples)

Process	Example rates	Comments
Text stage		
Development editing	£34.40 per hour Speed varies according to complexity, so a 10,000-word manuscript could cost £70–£230; 150,000 words £1,000–£3,500	This may be all the author ends up paying for if the report says substantial rewrites are required and they can't face it If the manuscript has been commented on by competent critics – and been through rewrites – then maybe this stage can be skipped
Copyediting	£29.90 per hour Speed varies according to the state of the manuscript, so 10,000 words could cost £60–£200; 150,000 words £900–£3,000	Many authors are unaware of the value of a style sheet or how to use Word styles, so a quick training session on consistency or headings could cut down on the time they have to pay for If there are references or copyright issues they haven't dealt with, that will cost extra
Proofreading (after design and layout)	See below	A common misconception among authors is that this is the stage they are coming to you for, which is why it is imperative you view the manuscript and give them an honest appraisal of the work that is needed

Process	Example rates	Comments
Copyright permissions	If the manuscript is heavily dependent on outside sources and specific illustrations then payment may have to be made to individual copyright holders and the bill can be huge There are professionals who deal with these in different fields (eg poetry; artwork; photography)	The editor's job is to flag up to the author that they have a legal obligation to acknowledge sources and to obtain permissions – just because an image or a quote comes up in an internet search does not mean it's free to use in another publication
Design and production stage		
ISBNs	In the UK, one ISBN costs £89 if bought singly but goes down to £16.40 or less if bought in bulk	Each format (hardback/paperback/ebook) requires a different ISBN and each territory has its own ISBN provider and fee level
Illustrators	From free for an author's own photos or family drawings to professionally crafted files at an average of £200+ per project	Including a substantial number of illustrations can increase production costs because of the work needed to make them suitable for print – they need to be CMYK and 300 dpi for colour or may need changing to grayscale to avoid the extra cost of colour printing; or they may need reformatting for ebook use Downloads from the internet should wave a red flag for copyright

Process	Example rates	Comments
Cover	Covers can be as simple and cheap or as complicated and expensive as the author wants There are free and paid-for photo libraries and cover designers charging a range of fees	A final cover can't be produced until the size of the book (height, width and number of pages) and what paper is being used are known; these dictate the spine width and can vary by several millimetres The back of the cover needs a blurb. Is the author writing it or are you, or should you suggest a marketing copywriter? Is there a logo to use, or does one need designing?
Barcode	Barcodes come free with some cover template services (IngramSpark and KDP) and there are many free barcode generation services It is unnecessary ever to pay for a barcode	These are essential if the book is going to be sold and must be in the right format and placed correctly The author can choose whether to include a price, but leaving it off means they can alter the pricing without redesign and re-uploading issues

Process	Example rates	Comments
Typesetting/ book layout	From free templates on some online platforms to £000s or £0,000s for bespoke design	There is a high level of frustration among first-time authors who thought it would be simple to upload a Word document and receive a beautiful book

Professionals will know what files are required by printers and for ebooks

Costs can be decreased by presenting a well-formatted Word manuscript and increased by introducing a high number of illustrations or tables |
| Indexing | £26.15 an hour, £2.95 a page or £7.90 per thousand words for an index to a non-academic text (Society of Indexers suggested rates in 2021) | Authors can produce lists as starting points for indexing, and InDesign, for instance, can produce an automatic index from selected words, but if the index is to serve the reader to its utmost there is no replacement for a trained indexer

Using indexing software that is not compatible with the layout software can add to time and cost |

2 | Assessing the author's needs

Process	Example rates	Comments
Proofreading	£25.70 per hour After a good copyedit and a straightforward typeset this should cost around £175 for 10,000 words and £2,500 for 150,000 words	Since elements can get lost in the typesetting process this stage is highly recommended This is often a stage that authors will undertake after typesetting, which is why the formatting work done at copyediting stage can be crucial
Ebook formatting	Service charges depend on the complexity and the provider (some are even free, but these may not handle images or unusual formatting) Files need to be validated but there are free online EPUB validators An image of the front cover needs to be made available in the right size for the sales platform	A first step is to produce an EPUB file (which can be done by the same person who typesets the print book, if there is one), then reformatting for different e-readers can be handled in many ways There are technical differences between reflowable and fixed formats and there are many tricks to sorting out how illustrations transfer, so the more layout dependent a publication is, the more expensive it will be to reformat
Audiobook production	Allow £2,000 to £4,000+ Some services charge per thousand words, others offer a package	Authors can do their own reading or hire a professional

Process	Example rates	Comments
Sales stage		
Print on demand	Services offer free accounts; authors can purchase copies at cost (as set by the provider) Costs of single books are fixed, but an ordinary paperback can be much cheaper than from a regular printer	Lulu and KDP don't charge for uploading book files IngramSpark do charge, but there are free promotions available, especially to ALLi members; and bookshops will buy from this system Any colour within the body of the book means the whole book will be costed as colour Recommend playing with cost calculators to work out the best size and format to use and to see if the retail price that needs to be charged is suitable for the market
Printing	It is always worth getting quotes from at least three printers as they can vary hugely; to give an accurate quote the printer needs to know the size of book, number of pages, type of paper, type of cover, whether the interior is going to be b&w or colour	Printers offer more flexibility on quality and design than through POD, but at a cost If they are not supplied with the right sort of PDF then they will charge for work that needs doing Unlike with POD, the position of colour pages can be managed to reduce printing costs

2 | Assessing the author's needs

Process	Example rates	Comments
Marketing and publicity	The person who is going to work hardest to sell the book is the author, who comes free but needs time and energy; a paid publicist can be expensive and offers uncertain rewards Leaflets, posters, bookmarks and other publicity items need designing and then printing at costs from £10+	The only way to build up interest (and therefore sales) is to be active, either by visiting bookshops and organisations relevant to the book or through social media and online book communities Whether an author needs marketing materials depends on how active they are and whether they are doing launches, talks or tours
Website and social media	Domain names from £0.99 From free hosting on some platforms to intricately designed websites for £000s or £0,000s and monthly or annual service charges Website costs should cover hosting, security features and the ability to make sales from the website Social media and Google offer a variety of ad packages Amazon offers free Author pages	Having an online presence is hugely important for book sales and sometimes a free social media presence (Facebook, Instagram etc) or a page on Amazon is not enough

Note: The ranges given for services are only indicative and an accurate quote should always be sought. Editing and proofreading figures come from CIEP **suggested minimum rates** in 2021

Author's timescale

It is possible to turn a manuscript into a book available on Amazon within a week. Whether it will be nice to look at, factually correct and enjoyable to read is another matter.

If the author has stated that they've done the proofread and just want it turned into a book then you can bet your bottom dollar that something is missing – refer to everything above and all the points to follow.

> I have yet to take on a self-publishing project that hasn't required at least one more thing the author wasn't aware of needing, and this can extend the timescale by weeks, even months.
>
> Editor and CIEP Advanced Professional Member

If they are at an even earlier stage and the manuscript isn't finished, there is no way you can predict how long it will be until they get 'the book'.

If the author doesn't respond to your queries, or if they supply you with inadequate material, or they decide that something has to be added or changed, then the timescale will extend. Don't promise delivery until you know what you're dealing with. But at all stages keep in touch about how long things are taking. As soon as you become aware of something that is going to impact the timescale (and probably the budget) then communicate with the author and offer them options.

Connecting with the author

The self-publishing road is heavily digital from start (writing programs) to finish (online sales sites) and you need to work out two things. First, is the author comfortable online and technically savvy? Second, are you technically compatible?

If the author is not happy with technical issues (such as using Track Changes or uploading files to online services) are you prepared to guide or to step in? Likewise, are you prepared to learn about software they rely on that is unfamiliar to you? If the answer is no – not even if you build the extra time into your fee – then it's probably best to admit that the project is not for you.

Talking the same language

If it is obvious that the author is a reluctant computer user, you'll need to avoid jargon and move on in simple steps. They may be used to basing communications on their mobile phone by sending instructions via WhatsApp or Messenger. You may receive swathes of text within emails rather than as document attachments. To avoid chaos you'll need to find a way to make sure that you at least don't lose information or your work. If you can suggest systems that your author takes up, so much the better.

If you are both, say, Microsoft Word and Dropbox users or Google Docs aficionados then agree protocols for information and file exchange, and look forward to a smooth electronic relationship. It's still worth exchanging a sample edit using Track Changes, just to check the process.

If the author is using software you've never even heard of, let alone tried, then you have the options of withdrawing politely or of seeing it as a CPD opportunity.

If you are working with a business you might be asked to use Google Docs, SharePoint, Slack or Microsoft Teams. These are just a few of the hubs designed for smooth file sharing, easy team chats and clear project management. Just make sure you get some training in the software, and check on the impact on your use of editing shortcuts, macros and so on.

Many authors invest in writing and designing programs such as Scrivener and Vellum, or they use the free word-processing package that came with their laptop. There are ways to convert in and out of Word, to and from these, but you need to be careful about effects on formatting, tracked changes and comments. Sending the author a PDF can avoid some problems, although this can make commenting tricky if they don't have the right software. A simple solution is to suggest they list comments on your work in a document or email, as long as it is clear what each comment refers to.

If your existing software or hardware or your broadband aren't up to heavy tech demands then you'll need to balance the value of the client against the cost of upgrading. But regularly upgrading your tech is part and parcel of being a professional editor.

Key questions when assessing an author

Table 5 is not a questionnaire for you to deliver in its entirety, neither is it comprehensive. It is a starter guide to obtaining a realistic picture of the author's work and what taking on the project might involve. The more experience you have with self-publishing authors the quicker you will pick up on how you can help them produce the best possible publication.

Table 5 Key questions when assessing an author

Question	Encouraging replies	More research needed
Is this your first book?	'No' – so they should be aware of many of the issues	'Yes' – you need to find out a lot more about their skills, knowledge and expectations
Who else has seen the manuscript?	'My partner/writing group/beta readers/editor' – the more outside input there's been, the closer the work will be to being editable, or even publishable	'Nobody' – then how do they know it has any merit? It might only be at development stage

Question	Encouraging replies	More research needed
Do you have a timescale in mind?	'After the editing then …' – they appreciate that the process is staged	'I want to upload it to KDP at the end of the month' – not a good sign if they're a first-time author; you need sight of the manuscript before committing to anything
Does it contain quotes from other sources?	'No' – nothing to worry about (unless you subsequently find some) 'Yes, I've followed Harvard referencing/I've checked they're out of copyright' – you'll need to build in checking time	'I got a lot of information from Wikipedia/each chapter begins with a TS Eliot quote' – you might need to explain about copyright rules or build in a fee for sorting out references
Is it illustrated?	'I've done my own' – no copyright issues, but there may be quality considerations	'A few from Wikipedia' – another query on copyright (and quality)
Who's the book for?	'Just my family' – content and production will create fewer considerations	'Everybody' – will they need handholding on how to publish or have they already opened POD accounts?
What's your budget?	'Whatever it takes' would be the dream response, but more often they are looking for quotes; at this point you can find out if they are aware of all the stages involved	'I don't have much money' – once you've seen the manuscript you'll be able to deliver a reality check

Question	Encouraging replies	More research needed
What formats are you thinking of?	'I want a paperback and an ebook'/'I just want an ebook' – indicates they are aware of the options; do you have the skill set to deliver for different formats?	'I want it on Amazon' – they may need introducing to the options and impacts of hardback vs paperback vs ebook
What software do you use? Are you familiar with Track Changes? Can you comment on PDFs?	'I use Word and am happy with Track Changes; I generally comment on PDFs in a Word document' – shows they are familiar with the software and you should connect smoothly	'I just use what came on my iPad; what's a PDF?' or 'I do all my writing in LaTex/Scrivener' – may indicate that you are on different technical levels, so one of you will have to be willing to learn and adjust

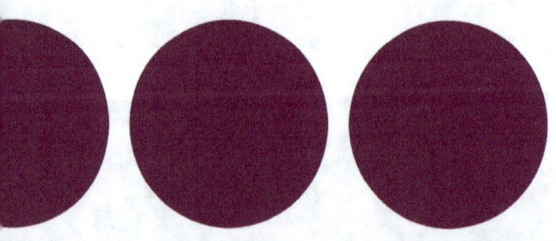

3 | The practicalities

Text preparation

Assessing a manuscript for editing level is a familiar process for any professional editor and should be carried out as part of your initial costing. Once you are working on the project you should be particularly stringent about formatting to smooth the transition to book design. If you are thinking of acquiring and offering typesetting skills then you could elide a few steps.

Accepting a manuscript

If your author has used writing software, such as Scrivener, then you need to be aware of the issues in transferring files. Scrivener's usefulness lies in the ease with which text can be located and moved around and how it helps to keep track, for example, of plot lines and characters in fiction or topics in factual books. Scrivener does export as PDF and Word files, but transfers to/from can lose Track Changes and alter formatting, sometimes because of the software, sometimes because of the user's lack of skill.

> I only use Scrivener for the very beginning and the very end of the book creation process. Scrivener does not handle red-lining well, which is critical for editors. I write the novel in Scrivener, export to Word, do critiques, a dev editor, copy editor, proofreader, and then import back into Scrivener for formatting.
>
> Amy Alton, self-publishing author, ALLi member Facebook discussion

Although Microsoft Word dominates the word-processing market there is a plethora of other document producers out there, from OpenOffice to Google Docs. So do check the file format that your author is using and then it will be a question of trial and error as to whether you can share files satisfactorily.

Writing software authors use

These are links to the programs most often referred to by self-publishing authors, which you might like to take a look at. Their reputations as accurate checkers of text are highly mixed among editors. If a client mentions their reliance on one, you could use a free trial offer to familiarise yourself with how it works and decide whether it will be a useful collaborative tool to invest in (from both a time and a money point of view). But most editors still work in Word and let the author do any reformatting.

- Ulysses was developed for Mac, iPad and iPhone – **ulysses.app**.
- Scrivener is a word processor, outliner and filing system for Windows and Mac –**literatureandlatte.com/scrivener**.
- Grammarly is an online 'writing assistant' – **grammarly.com**.
- ProWritingAid (PWA) is a 'writing coach' that integrates with a host of platforms – **prowritingaid.com**.
- Hemingway Editor is a free desktop app to improve web writing, which helps clarify prose – **hemingwayapp.com**.

> I've now got a lifetime PWA license. Grammarly is fine for basic or day-to-day stuff, but it's not advanced enough for professional writers. It also makes more errors than PWA. And it doesn't integrate so well with programs like Word and Scrivener.
>
> Kristina Adams, self-publishing author, ALLi member Facebook discussion

Which edit?

Ask the author about the amount of work and exposure their manuscript has undergone and whether anybody else has read it. After all, if it still needs a thorough development edit the author's timetable may need a review; or it may turn out not to be worth publishing; or they may not have sufficient funds for a 'proper' job.

Authors often think they just want a proofread, but you know that proofreading is what should happen after layout. Asking for a sample will help you judge whether the work is ready to be copyedited, or whether the author's dream of seeing their words between covers is still some way off.

3 | The practicalities

> I think authors aren't always clear about the different types of editing and the distinctions between them (eg developmental and copy editing and also proofreading), and I think it's important editors advise on the distinctions and maybe about which stage they're at and also if the work needs more self-editing before outsourcing it to an editor.
>
> Ellie Stevenson, self-publishing author, ALLi member Facebook discussion

As part of the copyediting process your first exchange may well be a list of queries, both general and specific, because you've unearthed text that reveals the need for referencing or further copy or something that impacts design. After that, record style decisions in the style sheet you should create as part of the editing process.

If you are going to apply Word styles at this stage, then do so without having Track Changes turned on. This lightens the load on the software and reduces the likelihood of it slowing or crashing. It is also a less horrific list for the author when they open your edited file.

If the manuscript is fiction then you'll need an appreciation of the genre's expectations, a handle on point of view, and an ability to gauge the strength of the characters and the plot logic. If the author can present you with a list of characters or a documented timeline then so much the better, but these may be documents you'll need to create so you can keep track of issues. You'll find a couple of useful books on fiction issues in '**Resources**', and there are many more out there. The **CIEP Introduction to Fiction Editing** course covers this in more detail.

If the manuscript is a biography or for business use then, over and above the language, your emphasis will be on creating an engaging reader experience with the logic of the layout and the completeness of the material. Among the likely issues to watch out for are: plagiarism; accurate referencing of sources; legal points that might arise due to libel, privacy or copyright; the need for tables and/or figures; missing data.

Content issues

The following are areas that traditional publishers have departments for. You are doing a self-publisher a service by flagging up any issues, but be sure to emphasise in your T&Cs/project contract that the author is ultimately responsible for all legal, copyright and reproduction issues.

Legalities

Avoid being drawn into potential liability for libel or violation of privacy; flag up any issues you find and make it quite clear to the author that they need to address them by consulting a lawyer or deleting the text.

Copyright

Copyright issues can arise in all genres and the CIEP course **Copyright for Editorial Professionals** is a good investment. You can also upgrade your skills with the **CIEP Referencing** course.

1. **Quotations:** Issues often arise because well-known lyrics or poems are commonly used as epigraphs linked to titles or chapter headings. Music in particular is a heavily copyrighted (and litigious) area, so you need to flag up any potential problems early. Many decisions on copyright are based on the principle of 'fair use', and using two lines from a haiku is the equivalent of using several chapters from a book, so care is needed. After all, if the author's whole premise is built

around a phrase they aren't going to be able to use, then thinking caps will need to go on. Money can get rid of many problems, but the cost of some permissions may be prohibitive.
2. **Information:** Issues here revolve around plagiarism and the proper acknowledgement of original sources. Check that the author is aware: a) that referencing needs to be done; b) of how to do it; c) that Wikipedia is not universally acknowledged as a prime source. If you have a suspicion that whole chunks of text have been copied and pasted (links/fields and non-breaking space markers are often indications) then there are plagiarism checkers (of different qualities) that can be put to use.
3. **Illustrations:** Query whether the author has received permission to use all the photos, diagrams or other illustrations in the manuscript. If they say they just downloaded them from Google, you must point out that does not automatically give them permission for use. Ask them to check the source and the licence.

Illustration quality

The use of illustrations creates extra cost, particularly if they need work (to improve quality or to make them good for different formats) and are in colour. It saves time if quality issues can be addressed before illustrations are needed for layout. This may be an area you can help with if you have the knowledge and the software (for instance, Adobe Photoshop and Illustrator).

If there are graphs and figures, you or the designer are likely to need access to the originals for editing because of misspellings or incorrect facts, or to impose consistency after styles have been decided. Titles or notes may need to be extracted from the image to appear in an in-text caption. Check the suffix of picture files as you may not have the software to open them (AI, EPS or TIFF files require the correct software; JPG is pretty universal and best for print; PNG is best for digital use).

Images are definitely not improved by being badly scanned or photographed. If a photo has been saved in a low resolution then there might be problems with pixellation – especially if they are enlarged. As picture files are copied from program to program, or if they are inserted into, for instance, Word or PowerPoint files, they lose quality. A low image quality might be unavoidable (for instance, if it is from historic archives), but there are ways to ameliorate originals. If the designer has access to them, so much the better.

If the author has produced a pencil drawing to show what they want, it is likely to need editing and properly producing, preferably by a professional illustrator. Light pencil lines do not reproduce strongly enough for print.

Formatting for layout

The key message you need to give your author on manuscript preparation is to keep it simple. Authors can get caught up in the visuals of their document, sometimes as part of the need to make sense of the flow, or just because they want to see what it looks like as a book. But it really doesn't matter whether the chapter headings are in **Bauhaus 93** or *Banshee*; the design stage is the time for those specifics.

If you can encourage authors to use only proper paragraph and character styles rather than adding manual formatting (such as applying bold from the ribbon) then that helps.

Typesetting programs read Word styles when importing, which reduces the margin for error and cuts down on time – for both typesetter and proofreader. It is part of a copyeditor's remit to mark up text for layout. Whereas you might insert tags for a traditional publisher, for a self-publisher it is best if you replace all the manual settings with 'proper' Word styles. CIEP's **Word for Practical Editing** course will fill in any gaps in your knowledge.

Using styles can be enough to make it clear which lines are chapter numbers/titles, which are headings, which paragraphs are blockquotes and so on. You may still need to use tags for some elements, particularly for figure captions and placements because they just need to be indicative – a typesetter needs some flexibility about where figures go during layout.

Imposing styles also helps to create an accurate and automatic table of contents (ToC). A ToC is useful at the editing stage for checking accuracy and completeness, but typesetters use styles to produce a new ToC after layout for accurate page numbering.

You can also point out to the author that by cleaning up the text formatting you are doing valuable preparation for ebook formatting or for using an automated print template service, such as KDP. A human typesetter can apply their knowledge and experience to interpreting oddities, but an automated program has no idea that what it has interpreted as, for instance, a chapter title is actually a subheading.

Since many self-publishers only produce ebooks, and ebook software can be very particular about formatting, you can really add value if you clean up a manuscript. For instance, by getting rid of double paragraph returns, unused styles, strange fonts, manual styling, hidden links or hyperlinks that don't work. Many an EPUB is rejected because of a quirky format or an unanchored image.

You've done your bit for design preparation if you've done your editorial best to do the following clean-up:

- Apply formal styles, so that, for instance, normal style is indented through the Style format and not by using a tab, or that there is a built-in page break before a chapter heading and not a series of the wrong type of break.
- Strip out manual styling by using the Clear Formatting function, revealed in the style bar when it shows a plus after the style name, for instance, 'Normal + 14pt', and replacing it with an existing or a newly created style to differentiate it from the body text.
- Remove excess spacing, as in two or more paragraph returns or double spaces after a full stop, or wrongly spaced punctuation.
- Indicate figure/table placement by using a tag system or by inserting a styled caption.

Anatomy of a book

You can help your author by clarifying with them:

- parts of a book they must have (the imprint/copyright page)
- parts the book might benefit from having (for instance a glossary or bibliography)
- how to produce specialist parts such as an index (and refer them to the Society of Indexers).

In brief:

- Each book should have preliminary pages, also called front matter or prelims – at a minimum these should be a title page and an imprint/copyright page (containing legally required information), and for factual books a table of contents.
- Added extras (some of which could go in the end matter) might be: a dedication, epigraph or quotation, acknowledgements; lists of illustrations, abbreviations, a glossary or notes on pronunciation; a preface, foreword and introduction; explanatory maps or diagrams; an author biography, reviews or list of other books.
- Typical end matter elements are: appendices; a bibliography or list of references or further reading; a glossary or an index; lists of credits and sources.

For a clear guide there's a free CIEP fact sheet on the anatomy of a book at **ciep.uk/resources/factsheets/#AB**.

Imprint page

In the UK it is a legal requirement that this page shows:

- the name and address of the publisher (which could just be Town, Country or a website address)
- details of the printer
- the author's copyright statement.

If your author is publishing in another country, you may need to help them check the equivalent requirements through their ISBN provider.

It is also the page to place cataloguing and marketing information. Options include:

- ISBNs (it could list all formats being produced, such as paperback, hardback, ebook, audiobook)
- the date of publication
- if it is a second or later edition, details of previous edition(s), such as dates or other ISBNs
- any bibliographic record information (for example, Cataloging in Publication or Library of Congress, or thema/keywords)
- credits for translators, illustrators, editors, indexers, designers
- credits for images and other items requiring permission to use
- notes on the materials used to produce the book (typefaces, paper)
- logo(s) of publisher, author etc.

Choosing a format

Before the edited manuscript is laid out as a book (or typeset) the author needs to decide on the format(s) they want to offer. Traditional publishers often issue a hardback first, followed by a paperback and an ebook, but the extra cost of producing a hardback means they are not always a self-publisher's first choice. There's a swathe of self-publishers who only produce ebooks – and they've developed quite active niches. Audiobook sales are growing and self-publishers are beginning to invest in the format.

Unless the author can research the requirements, is technically competent or is happy to invest in the right software and the training, then you should encourage them to use a professional to do the design and to produce the correct file formats for printers and for upload. They will avoid no end of frustration. But they need to be sure that the person they choose is not just a 'designer' but that they know about typesetting, about the end file requirements and about setting up the right cover template – because there are subtle differences, such as spine width or colour settings, which can lead to files being rejected.

If the author is happy to do it themselves then they will produce a better product if they invest in layout software, such as Vellum or InDesign, rather than rely on Word. If they are constrained by budget or skill then KDP does offer basic templates for Word files. These are generally aimed at simple novel layouts, while most non-fiction manuscripts are more complex (for instance, by including tables or an index). But the author must carefully read and rigidly stick to the well-specified requirements or they will still have upload troubles.

Hardbacks cost more and take more time to produce than paperbacks because of the nature of the cover. But the one text file can be used for both formats if the page size is the same – although different cover files will be needed.

Colour within the text (type or images) adds to the cost, because of both typesetting complexity and print cost.

Table 6 Format use and distribution

Format	Readers	Sales platforms	Notes
Printed book (paperback, hardback)	Universal	• Bookshops • Online retailers • Own website • Book tours	Investing in boxes of books can create logistical problems for distribution if the author hasn't got a specific sales outlet POD services mean that authors can now offer printed formats for minimal investment

Format	Readers	Sales platforms	Notes
Ebook	Those with e-readers, tablets, computers, mobile phones	• Online retailers • Own website	Many authors only produce an ebook, and concentrate on selling through KDP, but there are a host of other ways to distribute and offer different e-formats
Audiobook	Those with tablets, computers, mobile phones	• Online retailers (chiefly Audible) • Own website	A new market that has grown exponentially; requires either considerable investment or access to technical expertise, but independent services are penetrating the market and self-publishers are beginning to invest

Note: All formats are also available in libraries

Print on demand (POD) or traditional printer

The development of digital print machines opened up the publishing world. Digital printers don't need expensive, time-consuming, pre-press procedures (such as plate production); all they need is an electronic file (in the right format) and you can speedily produce one book or a hundred. Two major POD companies capitalised on this ease of production, KDP and IngramSpark, followed by their smaller cousin, Lulu – they all offer international distribution, but the first two are much larger. Of course, book pages still need binding inside a cover, which is why your average traditional printer likes to have a minimum order (often 20 books).

> ### Support service opportunity – being the 'publisher'
> If you have access to correctly formatted files, you could open your own POD account and be your author's 'publisher', which can work quite well for one-off books. You need to have the time to keep track of payments and forward them to the author (after a word with your accountant about the process).

Anybody can sign up for a free account with more than one POD company. In fact, many authors use KDP for ebooks and IngramSpark for print on the basis that Amazon Kindle dominates the ebook market and that bookshops and libraries will order through the systems IngramSpark has developed, but not via Amazon.

There is small print about taxes and copyright and payments that have to be agreed to, and card numbers that have to be given to cover publication costs. KDP doesn't charge for uploading files, IngramSpark does charge (but ALLi members get a number of free uploads). The unit cost of printing is dictated by the company but the account holder can decide on the retail prices for each global market. The companies have calculators so the author can work out whether the price they need to charge to cover costs and deliver some profit is actually suitable for the market they are aiming at. But be warned, once the book is out there it will be offered for sale at prices and by vendors over whom the author has no control. This is a constantly changing problem and another instance of the value of knowledge gained through ALLi membership from their published guides and by following posts on the members' Facebook page.

The author needs to check whether the size and format they want is available through the channel they've chosen. A traditional printer can produce a far wider range of designs than POD services, which offer limited options on trim size, book format and orientation, colour and type of paper. KDP and IngramSpark will generate a cover template, so the size of the spine is right for the number of pages and type of paper. IngramSpark automatically includes an ISBN barcode; KDP adds one afterwards if it is not already in the design.

The virtue of a POD account is that the book can be bought without the author having to invest in heavy boxes for which they have to find storage, run an ordering system and manage P&P. If they've got their marketing right, all they have to do is watch the 'publisher compensation' payments go into their bank account, 90 days after a sale.

So when an author says, 'I want to be on Amazon', this is the route they need pointing to. They need to open a POD account, load up the right files and type in the right metadata. If the author is a technophobe then you could offer an upload and metadata input service for those accounts that allow you access.

Using a POD service doesn't prevent the author from ordering a bulk print run from a regular printer for a specific event, or for volumes on higher-quality paper or thicker covers or more reliable colour reproduction. It is always worth comparing several print quotes, whatever the print run.

Support service opportunity – print contacts

If you have the contacts you could offer to collect print quotes, or give an author a list of printers to approach.

ebooks

This is the preferred, and often sole, format of many self-publishers. If they also want a paperback, it is usually typeset first and the file is then reformatted to produce an EPUB file – which needs to be validated (that is, pass a basic test for coding; see **Resources**).

One of the main complaints from authors who've done their own thing is that a Word document hasn't turned into a nice-looking ebook. This is because Word has input all sorts of code in the background that confuses the ebook formatting, which is why a new, stripped-down file must be produced. Remind your author that the design of an ebook is very different from a print book in that the reader has control over the size and type of font, while the reading device determines what typographical features show up and what don't. A carefully spaced print design with intricate formatting won't look the same in an ebook if it is not properly coded.

Ebooks have inbuilt procedures, such as ignoring double paragraph returns, not recognising fonts that aren't embedded, needing careful coding for indexes and showing images at the end of the text if they aren't anchored in the right location in the text flow. The best thing you can do as an editor is to strip out all extra spacing and to make sure that styles are correctly applied to everything, leaving no manual formatting. The ebook software will recognise correctly styled heading levels and some other styled text features, but if a chunk of normal text has been manually tweaked, the coding will see it as a normal paragraph.

If the book is mostly text then a **reflowable** EPUB is pretty simple to create. If the book is a masterpiece of design with text flowing round images, or carefully drawn up tables, then a **fixed layout** EPUB will be the answer, but it will need to be properly produced.

It is important to keep the file as small as possible, because the account holder is charged ebook download fees according to the size of the file. That means knowing how to reduce the size of included images while maintaining clarity.

For the technically competent there is plenty of software that converts documents to EPUBs, including InDesign, Vellum, Sigil, Calibre (free) and Jutoh. Companies that offer the service and remove much of the headache include Draft2Digital (free), Smashwords and BookFunnel.

Warn the author that, although they might set a retail price, ebook distributors can be a law unto themselves when it comes to final pricing and author royalties.

Audiobooks

This is a fast-developing market that indie authors are breaking into thanks to companies such as ACX and Findaway Voices. The major distributor is Amazon through Audible, but many authors use Findaway Voices services. There are authors with a recording background who are even doing their own file production.

Authors interested in this format should keep in touch with developments via ALLi. See **Resources** for contact recommendations.

About ISBNs

The role of ISBNs is one of the main questions self-publishers raise, and misunderstanding their use and technicalities can trip up authors who take an easy option and then find they want to develop their own publishing brand. If you can understand these details you can at least point your author in the right direction.

An International Standard Book Number identifies one title, in one edition/format. The grouped number sequence identifies the country of origin, the product type, the publisher or imprint and the specific edition/format. Once allocated to a publisher, they never expire and they are not transferable from one imprint to another.

ISBNs are used for purchasing, sales and stock control, and since they identify the publisher they can be useful for archive purposes. Allocating an ISBN is not part of ensuring an author's copyright, which generally rests automatically with the author – although different countries have different approaches. However, if the book is going to be publicly available and taken seriously then it needs an ISBN.

Figure 2 Elements of an ISBN[1]

If one title is going to be produced as a paperback, a hardback, an ebook and an audiobook – whether they are being distributed free or being sold – each format requires a unique ISBN. Once a title format has been allocated an ISBN it does *not* require a different one for a different country or for separate distributors.

Authors can acquire a 'free' ISBN through some platforms and self-publishing packagers, but this imposes limitations and that title is seen as being published by that platform. This may not matter if the title is a one-off with a limited market, the author is happy with the service and they receive income. However, if the author is not happy with the service then it is a bureaucratic nightmare to transfer the title.

[1] ISBN users' manual and FAQs documents can be downloaded from **isbn-international.org/content/isbn-users-manual**

3 | The practicalities

Be aware that KDP will allocate Amazon's own Standard Identification Number, or ASIN – although an author can use their own ISBN in the file upload information on KDP. ASINs are neither recognised nor used by the book-ordering databases that bookshops and libraries rely on. If the author has only used KDP and relied on the ASIN, but then wants to set up their own imprint, they will need to reissue their titles and formats with new ISBNs – and attempt to withdraw the old edition from KDP. This can cause all sorts of duplication and loss of revenue issues, which also applies to any ISBN bought from any other organisation. So warn your author about the danger of losing control and income.

If the author has plans for several formats, further titles and expansive marketing then you should advise them to register for their own ISBNs. Sourcing an ISBN requires some forward planning and account opening and the author has to be willing and able to engage with online systems.

Each country has its own ISBN issuer and bulk purchasing makes them cheaper. For instance, a single one costs $125 from Bowker (for the US) and £89 from Nielsen (for the UK); a package of ten, which is ideal for self-publishers planning several formats and more than one book, reduces the unit price to $29.50/£16.40.

If an author is going be a fully fledged self-publisher they will need to:

- decide on an imprint name
- register that name and take out a purchasing account with the relevant ISBN issuer (in the UK this is the Nielsen ISBN Store)
- purchase a chunk of ISBNs, which do not have an expiry date and belong to that imprint in perpetuity
- register individual, allocated ISBNs with the issuing authority (which in the UK means having a separate Nielsen Title Editor account), which is done after design, because the registration needs to carry such metadata as size and number of pages
- fulfil any legal deposit obligations after registration; each country has its own legal deposit system – in the UK you need to supply six copies of each title format, in the US it is two and in Australia there are federal and state requirements.

Note: Serial publications (journals and newspapers) do not require an ISBN but do use ISSNs (International Standard Serial Numbers) for cataloguing and referencing. In the UK these are free from the British Library (full information at **bl.uk/help/get-an-isbn-or-issn-for-your-publication#**).

> ### Support service opportunity – towards packaging
>
> Some authors appreciate help with registering their ISBNs and are happy to give access to their account. If you get to grips with the metadata required to register an ISBN then you could add this service to your portfolio.
>
> If you find yourself working with many one-off self-publishers – and you have access to the correct file formats for upload – then you could consider taking steps towards becoming a project manager – or mini-packager. The first step would be choosing an imprint name and purchasing ISBNs in bulk from your regional provider. You would then be the 'publisher' for authors who aren't comfortable online or who only need one or two ISBNs.

About metadata

This is the book world's equivalent of SEO (search engine optimisation). It's the basic information used to describe and sell the book. There are a minimum of 20 fields that need to be filled in when registering an ISBN. These cover the fundamentals (book title and subtitle, author, illustrator, ISBN, format, number of pages, number and type of illustrations, publication date, price) and the sales and marketing descriptors (long and short book description, author biography, audience target, content categories, specialist subjects, keywords).

Point your author at a recognised classification system to choose one main code and three subsidiary codes (see **Resources**). Then recommend they set out all the information in a separate document so it is to hand when registering an ISBN, when uploading files or even when doing some marketing.

IngramSpark and ALLi offer advice on how to optimise metadata to make the book stand out. Active book marketers tweak their metadata as they discover more about their audience and sales.

Book distribution

Books will only be looked for if buyers know about them, but they do have to be easily found.

Print books

Unless the book has an ISBN, it won't get on the book databases that bookshops (and libraries) order from.

IngramSpark has a relationship with the main international book distributors, which is why an IngramSpark account is worth having, because bookshops and libraries can locate and order your ISBN.

Amazon's method of giving a book published through KDP an ASIN means bookshops and libraries can't find them on their databases and so won't order them.

Authors often feel that the holy grail is to see their book in Waterstones and WHSmith. Both these organisations have fixed ways of buying books and unless the author has a personal relationship with their local branch manager they'll be directed to Head Office or to a major distributor, such as Gardners.

The other holy grail is seeing a book *on* Amazon, which doesn't mean the author has to publish *with* Amazon. Files uploaded to IngramSpark will appear on Amazon, as well as being sold via other online distributors, such as Book Depository.

ebooks

If the author is only publishing an ebook then using KDP alone might be their best bet – but authors don't have full control over pricing and availability. IngramSpark will distribute ebooks, but doesn't claim it as a forte.

Many authors swear by Draft2Digital and Smashwords, but it is a fluid space and new systems are coming online all the time.

Technically minded authors might enjoy the facilities offered by BookFunnel for managing ebook marketing, distribution and sales on their own website.

4 | Additional professional services

If an author needs to source any of the following services they should go to the relevant professional body and check for a membership directory. Author social media groups are a good source of recommendations. This is also an area where ALLi membership is invaluable. ALLi vets approved partners for their database – and has a warning system about service providers who have been found wanting.

Some of these roles might be ones you could adopt to expand your business, but do be sure to acquire the right technical knowledge. Or team up with experts to offer complete solutions to self-publishers.

Indexers

> **Support service opportunity – indexing**
> Many CIEP members are also professional indexers, and if you think the skill set might be a good fit for your business then explore the **Society of Indexers** for more information and training.

An index is normally not needed in fiction, but it can be extremely useful in a biography and one is pretty much essential for non-fiction and business books.

An index for a print book can only be produced once the tome is typeset because it needs to carry page numbers. It is commonly thought that ebooks don't need them because of full-text searching. However, a true index is more than just a list of names or terms, so they can, and do, exist in ebooks. The software is constantly adapting and updating.

Authors often feel they are best placed to produce an index, or may not have the money to pay for the service. Their most useful contribution can be to list those names and terms they want people to find, which can be used to produce a simple, single-level index. Word and InDesign do offer indexing features that can handle levels of indexing but, as the Society of Indexers (SI) says on its website:

> Indexes are essential to almost any non-fiction book. They are often the first point of reference for the reader, and will be the most efficient route to finding specific information in the book. Books without indexes can be frustrating for the user, and information in the text can easily be missed.
>
> The skill of indexing lies in analysing the document, identifying indexable terms and concepts, and creating appropriate headings. The indexer needs to be able to anticipate the needs of the user in finding suitable entry points … Professional indexers use specialised software to automate the mechanical aspects of the job, but the intellectual task of selecting appropriate terms for index entries, and deciding what is significant information in a text, can only be done by a human indexer.

If the author is going to use a professional indexer then suggest they get the typesetter and indexer to liaise about the time-consuming technicalities.

> My advice for self-publishers would be:
> – do not embed index entries if the book is to be typeset (except perhaps as a reminder or basis to start compiling a manual index); create an index the old-fashioned way, and provide it as a Word file.
> – if the book will be an e-publication and won't be typeset (eg direct conversion of a Word file) and a simple index without subentries or page ranges will suffice, then Word's index feature can be used, but check that the software preserves the embedded index.
> Basically, we've two worlds – design/setting and word processing – and automated features from the latter are often incompatible or too simple for the former.
>
> Rich Cutler, CIEP Advanced Professional Member

4 | Additional professional services

Illustrators/cover designers

> **Support service opportunity – photo-editing**
> If you have photo-editing software, time and knowledge then you could deploy it here – especially if the author is unable to reformat appropriately or is no longer able to use the original illustrator.

Interior pictures

It is never all right to download and use random pictures from the internet, even if the quality is good enough. Even those websites that offer free illustrations can impose limits on commercial use. If the author is using other people's material they must get permission.

If the author commissions a professional illustrator they need to be clear about the licence they are buying. Many illustrators hang on to an element of ownership, and sole use can be expensive. So the picture the author bought of their central character may need to be re-bought if they want to use it on promotional items (say a toy or a T-shirt). **The Association of Illustrators** offers contract advice.

If the illustrator is not also the typesetter then the files they produce need to be sent in an image file format that suits the medium they are being published in (CMYK for print, RGB for ebook), or that can be manipulated by the typesetter. If images are inserted in a PowerPoint or saved as the wrong sort of PDF, then extracting the actual image can be a nightmare.

Home-produced illustrations can also present file download, editing and reproduction issues.

Covers

Many will say that creating a good cover is one of the dark arts. The cover is effectively the author's shop window, so it has to be good and right for the genre if it is going to sell the book. That usually means an author's best option is to use a professional cover designer, rather than one of the myriad cheap offers via a bidding site or producing one themself using a free photo.

For inspiration, an author only needs to trawl bookselling or reader sites to see what the competition's covers are like. Amazon's product details show a book's sales ranking (overall and by genre), which may give some indication as to whether a cover design is working. The author needs to bear in mind that the final image will need to work as a thumbnail if it is going to appear online.

Authors often commission a cover design before they've decided on the book trim size, but getting a cheap, online cover designer to change things isn't always easy. They need to check they can tweak the image to fit the final cover template. KDP offers cover templates as a PDF or as a PNG file and adds a barcode in a designated spot afterwards. IngramSpark supplies templates as a PDF or an InDesign file and adds a barcode that the cover designer can move and resize to suit. But the downloaded templates will only have the correct spine width if the final number of pages and the paper type is input – that is, after the book has been laid out.

Many an author gets frustrated at the file upload stage with KDP or IngramSpark because of subtle problems with the cover: titles or ISBNs don't match the metadata; the spine width is wrong; the image doesn't bleed correctly; the type just touches or spills over the inner margin. For a trouble-free experience they must begin by reading the company's guidelines and then follow the instructions. If they don't understand a term (such as bleed or CMYK) there is plenty of help on the internet.

If a book is also going to a traditional printer, then spine widths may change, depending on the paper and binding process, which may require a cover design tweak.

Generally, the cover should be produced as a separate file from the interior. Some printers, particularly for small booklets, will want the cover inserted into the main print file as the first and last pages.

Book layout

> **Support service opportunity – layout**
>
> If you have the skills and interest then invest in InDesign and some training and add layout to your professional services offering.

As the self-publishing industry grows so does the range of do-it-yourself layout offerings. If you google 'book design template' you get well over 700,000 results, some offering templates for Word, others for InDesign and so on. There are also tools that import a manuscript into a template and produce a PDF for printing. Vellum is software that many self-publishers purchase and swear by. Adobe InDesign is the industry standard software that offers maximum flexibility (with the older QuarkXPress also a contender). Many online services offer a limited range of templates with restricted ability to adapt.

There are many subtleties to laying out a book and to making it a pleasure to read and easy to use. These include font choice, margins, tracking, placement of headers and footers, styling of table of contents and indexes, and much more. So whether a service provider calls themselves a designer or a typesetter, the important thing is that they understand and apply the nuances.

If the author is happy to pay a professional then direct them to the **CIEP Directory** or to recommendations from ALLi.

Marketing and publicity

> **Support service opportunity – publicity**
>
> If you are an editor with social media or copywriting skills then you might be worth your weight in gold to an author who just wants to concentrate on writing books!

No marketing, no sales. If the author is publishing to make money then they won't sell their book unless they are prepared to throw themselves into social media, book launches and tours, or even do some advertising.

If the author is finding it difficult to devise a pithy blurb to describe their book, or is planning an extensive marketing campaign, then it might be worth employing a professional copywriter.

Publicity is hard work and if you know a good publicist then forming a partnership with them might be an offering an author would find very attractive.

Agents

If the author wants an agent then they aren't a self-publisher and they should invest in a copy of the *Writers' and Artists' Yearbook* and plenty of time to carry out the right research – but that is well beyond the remit of this guide.

5 | Resources

Audiobook production
Amazon's ACX for Audible **acx.com**

Findaway Voices **findaway.com**

Barcode services
Sold by Nielsen, offered for free on cover templates from KDP and IS. Many free generators available on the web. Among those recommended by self-publishers are:

Bookow **bookow.com/resources**

Ean-13 barcode generator **free-barcode-generator.net/ean-13**

Book and ebook design (and distribution)
Adobe InDesign (all-singing, all-dancing industry software, available on Creative Cloud subscription, converts to EPUB) **adobe.com**

BookFunnel (delivering ebooks in all formats and other marketing tools) **bookfunnel.com**

Calibre (free, open-source and much-loved tool for organising, viewing, editing and formatting ebooks) **calibre-ebook.com**

Draft2Digital (self-publishing design and distribution service) **draft2digital.com**

eBookIt! (ebook publishing service that offers a free EPUB validation service) **ebookit.com**

Jutoh (digital publishing specialist, one-off purchase) **jutoh.com**

Pagina (downloadable EPUB validation tool) **pagina.gmbh**

Sigil (multiplatform ebook editor based on open-source software, for the more technically minded) **sigil-ebook.com**

Smashwords (specialist indie ebook formatter and distributor, a free platform) **smashwords.com**

Vellum (for Mac users only, loved by fiction authors for speed and ease of amendments, its templates have limitations when dealing with illustrations and tables, converts to EPUB) **vellum.pub**

CIEP

Suggested CIEP guides

ciep.uk/resources/guides

Editorial Project Management

Pricing a Project: How to prepare a professional quotation

Suggested CIEP courses

ciep.uk/training/choose-a-course

Copyright for Editorial Professionals

Editing Digital Content

Editorial Project Management

Efficient Editing: Strategies and Tactics webinar

References

Word for Practical Editing

Illustration/cover design software

Adobe Creative Cloud (InDesign/Photoshop/Illustrator) **adobe.com**

Affinity Designer **affinity.serif.com**

Book Brush **bookbrush.com**

Canva **canva.com**

GIMP.org for Windows **gimp.org**

ISBNs

Bowker (official source for US and Australian ISBNs) **isbn.org**; Bowker's tools, advice and resources for self-publishers **selfpublishedauthor.com**

British Library (for free ISSNs for serial publications) **bl.uk/help/get-an-isbn-or-issn-for-your-publication#**

International ISBN Agency (for general information and to locate a local agency) **isbn-international.org**

Nielsen Book (runs the ISBN Agency for the UK and Ireland), purchases from **nielsenisbnstore.com** and registering title data on **nielsentitleeditor.com**

Metadata

BIC Subject Categories and Qualifiers **ns.editeur.org/bic_categories**

IngramSpark blog 'Facts About Book Metadata and Why It's Critical to Your Publishing Success' **ingramspark.com/blog/7-facts-about-book-metadata**

Thema Subject Categories 1.4 **ns.editeur.org/thema**

Plagiarism checkers

Duplichecker (some free tools, some plans) **duplichecker.com**

Plagiarism Detector (free for up to 25,000 words) **plagiarismdetector.net**

Plagramme (free quick check) **plagramme.com**

PlagScan by Ouriginal (free 2,000-word trial then a range of packages) **plagscan.com**

Quetext (free for 2,500 words) **quetext.com**

Print on demand and book distribution/sales

Amazon's KDP **kdp.amazon.com**

Draft2Digital **draft2digital.com**

Gardners **gardners.com**

IngramSpark **ingramspark.com**

Lulu **lulu.com**

Useful books

Bradburn, R (2020). *Self-Editing for Self-Publishers: Incorporating a style guide for fiction*. Skibbereen, West Cork: Reen Publishing (ISBN 9781838016500 and Kindle)

Mitchell, M and Wightman, S (2017). *Typographic Style Handbook*. London: MacLehose Press (ISBNs pb 9780857057532; ebk 9780857057525)

Writers' & Artists' Yearbook **bloomsbury.com**

Useful organisations

Alliance of Independent Authors (ALLi) **allianceindependentauthors.org**

Association of Illustrators **theaoi.com**

IPG, Independent Publishers Guild **independentpublishersguild.com**

PLSclear (fast-track service linking to publishers' permission departments) **plsclear.com**

ProCopywriters, the Alliance of Commercial Writers **procopywriters.co.uk**

Society of Authors **societyofauthors.org**

Society of Indexers (SI) **indexers.org.uk**. Download
Last but not least: a guide for editors commissioning indexes

About the author

Alison Shakspeare learnt her first editing and design lessons in London's theatre world before starting her own arts marketing consultancy, which metamorphosed into Shakspeare Editorial after training with the CIEP, of which she is an Advanced Professional Member. That she can offer a mix of editing and creative design to help self-publishers produce as professional a book as possible is as perfect a work state as she can imagine.

ShakspeareEditorial.org

Acknowledgements

This guide grew out of the trust placed in me by the growing band of independent authors whose various manuscripts I helped launch into the wider world. Their needs gave me the impetus to grow my service portfolio. But without the CIEP and its members – the training, the sharing of knowledge, the passing on of contacts – none of that would have been possible.

Thank you to Margaret Hunter for seeing the possibilities in a guide like this, and to her support team of editors. Thanks too to the beta readers, Lesley Wyldbore and Lisa Cordaro, who helped me hone the messages.

Alison Shakspeare

www.ingramcontent.com/pod-product-compliance
Lightning Source LLC
Chambersburg PA
CBHW071800080526
44588CB00013B/2313